Sally

Lehrwerk für den
Englischunterricht ab Klasse 3

Pupil's Book 3

Ausgabe Bayern

Erarbeitet von
Martina Bredenbröcker, Würzburg
Jasmin Brune, Sonsbeck
Daniela Elsner, Frankfurt/Main
Barbara Gleich, Uhingen
Stefanie Gleixner-Weyrauch, München
Simone Gutwerk, Würzburg
Marion Lugauer, Erding
Sabine Schwarz, Winsen/Luhe
Anke Spangenberg, Kiel

Unter Beratung von
Jane Brockmann-Fairchild, Bidingen

Illustriert von
Barbara Jung, Wilfried Poll,
Anja Boretzki, Gisela Vogel

Oldenbourg Schulbuchverlag, München

Inhalt (★ Unit optional)

pupil's CD / teacher's CD
teacher's CD only
Sally's task
★ extra
Work with a partner.
Work in groups.
Think. Pair. Share.
Write.
Draw.
Speak.

The happy kangaroo song

1 **Listen and sing.**

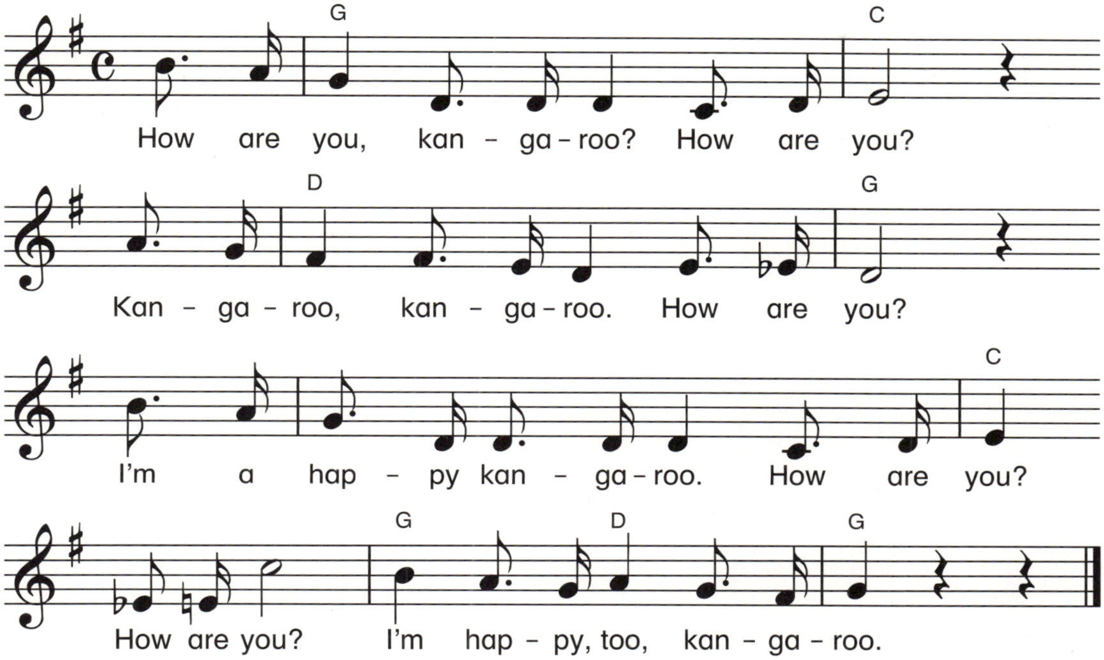

2 **Ask your partner:** What's your name? How are you?

English all around

1 **There are many English words in the picture.**
Look and say: I can see …

2 **Think. Pair. Share.**
Which other English words do you know?

3 Make a poster with English words.
Cut out pictures or words from magazines.

4 Think. Pair. Share.
Group the words (sports, food, drinks, ...).

Mr Blue and Mrs Yellow

1 **Listen and point.**

- blue
- yellow
- green

2 **What colour is it?**

- grey
- pink
- orange
- purple
- brown
- red
- white
- black

3 **Act out the story with a partner.**

CD 1.4

Sally's rhyme

1 Listen, say the rhyme and do the actions.

1, 2, 3 –
Sally, point to me!

4, 5, 6 –
Sally, let us mix!

7, 8, 9 –
now let's stand in line!

Now comes 10,
let's say the rhyme again!

2 Learn the rhyme.

3 Say the numbers from 1 to 10.

In class

1 **Listen and point.**

2 **What school things have you got?**
I've got a ...

Make your own picture dictionary. Draw. Read, look up and write down.

 CD 1.12

School in England

I can see …

On the photo, I can see …

1 Talk about the photos.

in the classroom

pupils in school uniform

lunchtime

a lollipop lady

2 Listen and read.

Hello, my name is Ella. I'm 9.
I go to Westminster School. I'm in class 3c.
My teacher is Mrs Black.
My school uniform is red and white.
School starts at 9 o'clock in the morning
and ends at 4 o'clock in the afternoon.
I like music and sports.
What about you?

3 What about your school day? Do a presentation.

Checkpoint 1

schoolbag	pencil	
book	rubber	pen

blue	red	black	yellow	green
grey	pink	brown	orange	white

1 **Look and speak.**

2 **What colours do you like?** I like …

Compare the words in English and German:
blue – blau, green – grün, ...

- Ich kann jemanden auf Englisch begrüßen.
- Ich kann jemanden nach dem Namen fragen.
- Ich kann mich vorstellen.
- Ich kann Farben nennen und danach fragen.
- Ich kann Schulsachen benennen.

Head and shoulders

1 Sing the song and do the actions.

2 Sing the song faster and faster.

3 Sing and drop the word head.
Sing again and drop the words head and shoulders ...

Ouch!

1 **Read the comic.**

Glad monster, sad monster

happy

sad

scared

angry

tired

1 **Listen, point and say:** The yellow monster is …

2 **Draw your own monster and write.** My monster is …

Snakes and ladders

1 Play the game. Do the actions.

Roll the dice. Do the cctions.

Correct action 🙂: Go up the ladder.

Wrong action 🙁: Go down the snake.

Sally's hotspot:

Correct action 🙂: Roll the dice again.

Wrong action 🙁: Go back to the start.

3 Touch your head.

8 Bend your knees.

16 Sing: Head and shoulders …

19 Wash your hands.

24 Count your fingers.

27 Shake your feet.

29 Stretch your arms.

33 Point to your eyes.

43 Touch your ears.

48 Stretch your legs.

52 Brush your hair.

58 Say: Good morning!

59 Point to your nose.

62 Shake your body.

The fish who could wish

In the deep blue sea,
in the deep of the blue,
swam a fish who could wish,
and each wish would come true.

He wished for a castle.

He wished for a car.

He wished for a horse and a Spanish guitar.

One day, just for fun, that silly old fish,
wished the silliest, silliest wish he could wish.

That silly old fish wished he could be
just like all the other fish in the sea.

But wishing was something other fish could not do.
So that was his very last wish that came true.

1 **Listen and point.**

2 **Look at the pictures.**
Tell the story to your partner.

 CD 1.23

Tim's wish list

1 **Look at the toys. What does Tim want? Tell your partner:**
Tim wants a bike ...

2 **Ask your partner:** How much is the ...?

3 **Make a wish list for your class and talk about it. Use your dictionary. Read, look up and write down.**
We want ...

Sally in the snow

1 **Listen to the story.**

2 **Look and say:** Sally puts on her … / Sally takes off her …

3 **What are you wearing?**
Read, look up and write down.
I'm wearing …

dress · shirt · shoes · jeans · pullover…

What's the weather like?

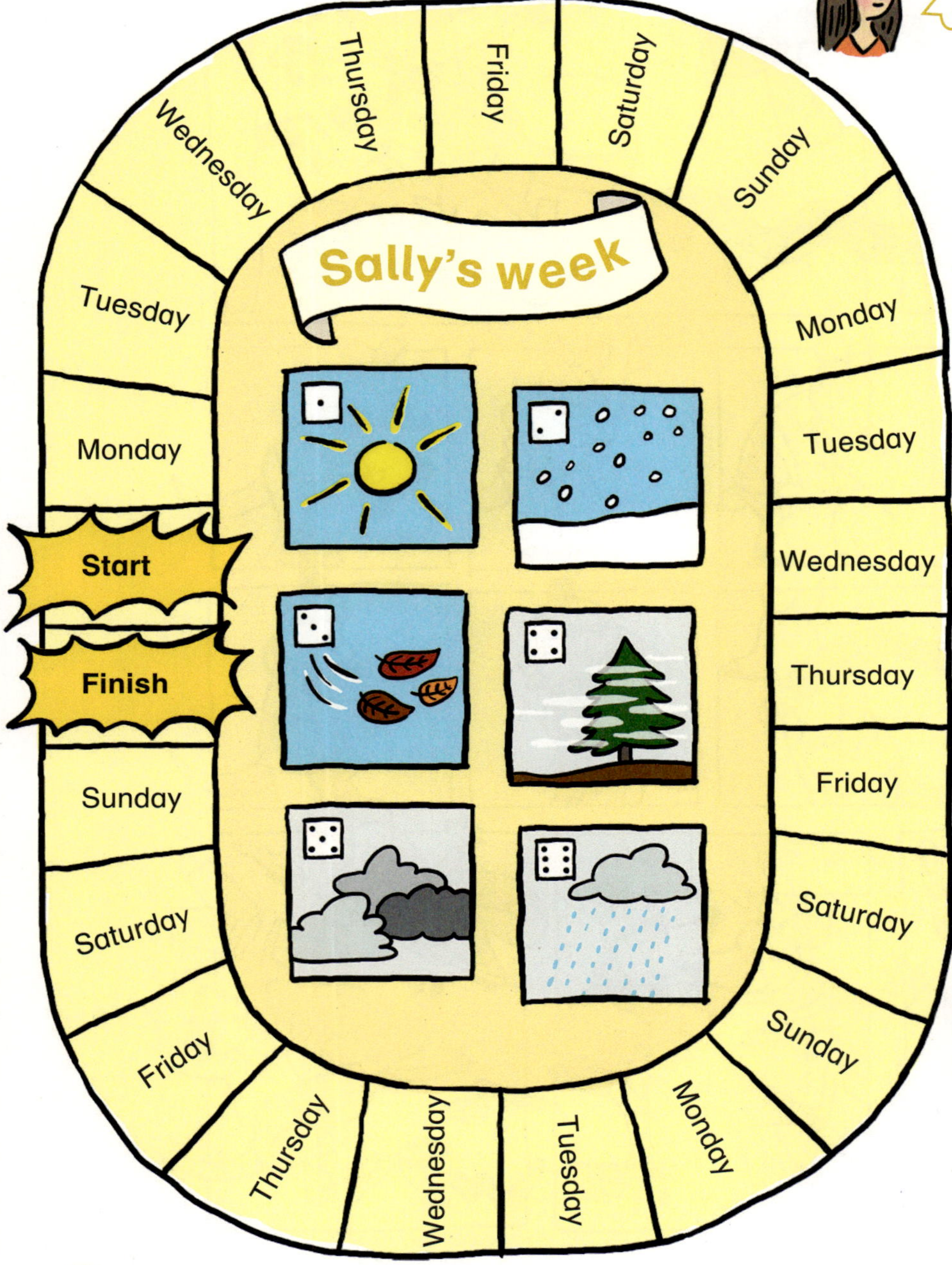

What day is it?

It's Monday (Tuesday...).

What's the weather like?

It's snowy and cold (sunny and hot ...).

On Monday, it's snowy and cold.

1 Play the game:
Roll the dice: What day is it? – It's Monday (Tuesday...).
Roll the dice again: What's the weather like? –
It's snowy and cold (sunny and hot...). – On Monday, it's snowy and cold.

The weather forecast

1 **Talk about the picture:** I can see …

2 **What's the weather like? Listen, point and tell.**

3 **What's the weather like in Paris, in Hamburg …?**
Look in a newspaper or on the Internet.
Make a weather forecast in your group and do a presentation.

Presentation tips:
- Speak loudly and clearly.
- Look at the class.
- Show pictures.

Make a weather chart for one week.
On Monday, it's cold / hot …

Checkpoint 2

happy fine okay sad

doll football book bike racing car helicopter spaceship

1 **Look and speak.**

2 **What are you wearing?** I'm wearing …

dress jeans pullover shirt shoes socks trousers skirt

Compare the words in English and German:
1 arm – 2 arms, 1 Arm – 2 Arme

- ✓ Ich kann auf Englisch sagen, wie ich mich fühle.
- ✓ Ich kann sagen, welches Spielzeug ich möchte.
- ✓ Ich kann fragen und sagen, wie viel etwas kostet.
- ✓ Ich kann sagen, welche Kleidung ich anhabe.
- ✓ Ich kann einige Körperteile benennen.

Emily's birthday party

1 **Talk about the picture:** I can see …

2 **How do you celebrate your birthday?**

3 **Make a birthday calendar.**

4 **Write a birthday invitation.**

Keith Haring

the artist

"Best buddies"

"Football"

"Group"

1 **Look at the pictures.**
Talk about the colours and actions:
I can see ...

2 **Find out and learn about Keith Haring on the Internet.**

friend	orange	red
blue	purple	yellow
play football	dance	

Working together

Doing a presentation

"Dancing in the sun"

"Friends"

3 **Make a picture about friends:**

1. Cut out different figures.
2. Glue them on coloured paper.
3. Trace your figures with a black pen.

My family

1 Look and point.

my mum and dad

my brother Tim

my grandma and grandpa

Can you find my grandma and grandpa?

aunt Helen

Can you find my mum and Tim?

Can you find aunt Helen?

2 Read the rhyme.

My father, my mother,
my sister, my brother,
the baby and me.
Oh, what a big family.

What is it?

tea, coke, orange juice, coffee, hot chocolate, milk

1 Look and guess.

At the drinks stand

2 Look and read.

3 Make your own drinks stand. Act out the scene.

4 Make a poster about drinks.

My favourite breakfast

everyday breakfast

traditional cooked breakfast

1 Look and speak.

Do you like

on your
in your

?

2 Ask your partner.

3 What do you have for breakfast? Write.

For breakfast, I have ...

milk coffee tea water hot chocolate orange juice toast roll
bread butter cheese egg ham honey jam cornflakes

1 **Look and speak.**

2 **How many brothers and sisters have you got?**
I've got … / I haven't got …

3 **What do you have for breakfast?**
For breakfast, I have …

bread	butter	cheese	eggs
ham	tea	water	hot chocolate

Compare the words in English and German: January – Januar, …

- Ich kann auf Englisch sagen, wann mein Geburtstag ist.
- Ich kann jemanden nach seinem Alter fragen.
- Ich kann jemandem zum Geburtstag gratulieren.
- Ich kann fragen, wie viele Geschwister jemand hat.
- Ich kann meine Familie und Freunde beschreiben.
- Ich kann sagen, was ich frühstücke.

At the ice cream stand

1 Listen and speak.

2 Make a word web with fruit words. Use your dictionary.

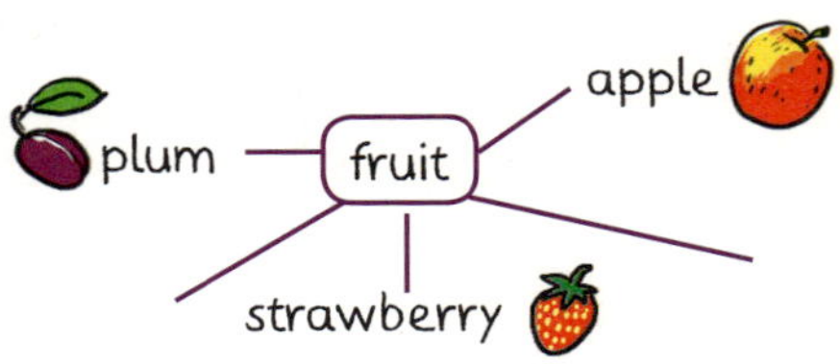

3 Ask your partner:
What's your favourite ice cream?

Let's make a smoothie

1 Look and read.

This is what you need.

Wash the strawberries.

Peel the bananas.

Cut the fruit.

Put them into the jug.

Add water or milk.

Mix it.

Pour the smoothie into your glass.

Enjoy!

2 Make your own smoothie.

Little dog lost

1 Listen. Where is Bobby?

 CD 2.7

These pets have new homes

Jack and Mr Tailor

Hopsy and Sophie Miller

Tippy and Mrs Davis

Molly and Kevin Fisher

Fred and Alice Smith

Rocky and Sammy Baker

Charlie and Mrs Cooper

1 **Listen, look and speak.**

2 **Make a missing pet report. Use your dictionary.**

3 **Act it out with your partner.**

Speedy

The wheels on the bus

1. The wheels on the bus go round and round,
round and round, round and round.
The wheels on the bus go round and round,
all around the town.

2. The wipers on the bus
go "Swish, swish, swish" …

3. The horn on the bus goes "Beep, beep, beep" …

4. The money on the bus goes "Clink, clink, clink" …

5. The driver on the bus says "Move on back!" …

6. The baby on the bus says "Wah, wah, wah!" …

7. The mummy on the bus says "Shh, shh, shh" …

1 Listen, sing and act it out.

Write your own verse. Use your dictionary.

Let's go to London!

the Royal Family

guards

Buckingham Palace

Tower Bridge

the London Eye

Big Ben

1 **Look at the photos.**

2  **Make a poster about London sights. Find out and learn about London sights on the Internet.**

Clumsy the dog

1 Listen to the story.

2 Read the story.

horse cow pig hen

Alphabet rhyme

A B C D E F G,
on the farm there is a bee.

H I J K L M N,
it lands directly on a hen.

O P Q R S T U,
and asks her friendly:
"How are you?"

V W X Y Z,
"I'm fine, but please,
get off my head."

1 **Listen and point.**

2 **Read the rhyme.**

1 **Look and speak.**

2 **What's your favourite pet?**
My favourite pet is a … Its name is …
It's …

cat	dog	fish	hamster
mouse	rabbit	guinea pig	

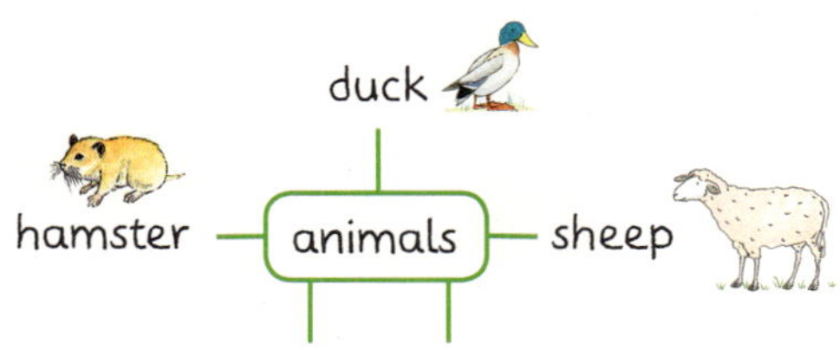

3 **Write a word web with animal words.**
Use your word list.

Compare the words in English and German: 1 horse – 2 horses, 1 Pferd – 2 Pferde

- Ich kann auf Englisch Obstsorten benennen.
- Ich kann ein Eis bestellen.
- Ich kann einige Tiere benennen und beschreiben.

Robin Hood's game

1 **Play the game.**

Robin Hood
Look!
The sheriff is coming.
Go to 16.
16
17
18
19
20
21
22
23
Have breakfast
on the farm.
Miss a turn.
Wave to the farmer.
Go to 37.
34
35
36
33
37
32
Drink some milk.
Go to 34.
38
Hide
behind
the tree.
Go to 19.
ook at
he castle.
oll the dice again.
31
39
30
29
28
27
40
41
Give money to the poor.
Go to 31.
42
FINISH

Rush hour

The ghost

I saw a ghost.
He saw me, too.
I waved at him.
But he said "Boo!".

Tongue twister

2 witches are watching 2 watches.
Which witch is watching which watch?

1 **Look and read.**
Can you say the tongue twister?

Choose a witch and describe her to your partner:
My witch is … Her hair is … orange yellow grey brown

It's Halloween

1 Listen to the song.

2 Listen to the story.

Act out the story.

Christmas Eve

1 **Look and find these Christmas things:**
mistletoe, Christmas tree, stockings, Christmas cards, presents

2  **Listen to the story.**

3  **How do you celebrate Christmas?**

 CD 2.29

I hear them

1 Listen to the song.

2 Sing the song.

3 Act out the song.

4 Make a Christmas card.

5 Read the rhyme.

Here are the reindeer.
Here is the chimney.
Here is the top.
On Christmas evening –
down Santa will drop.

CD 2.34

Make your own Christmas stocking

You need:
thick brown paper, a pencil, scissors, glue, a hole punch, wool, felt tips or wax crayons and coloured paper

Draw a large stocking on the thick brown paper.
Cut out 2 copies of the stocking.

Glue the 2 stockings together around the edges.
Leave the top open.

Punch holes around the edges of the stocking.
Weave wool in and out of the holes.

Leave a loop of wool.
Tie it into a knot.
Decorate your stocking.

1 Look and read.

2 Create your own stocking.

Describe your stocking: On my stocking there is/are …

star tree
candle

Valentine's cards

1 Read the comic.

2 Read the rhymes. What's your favourite rhyme?

Candy is sweet,
this is true,
but for my Valentine
I'll choose you.

Jingle, jangle,
silver bangle,
you look fit
from every angle.

3 Make your own Valentine's card.

Edgar's Easter eggs

1 Listen to the story. Act it out.

2 Where are the Easter eggs? Look and tell.

in on under
behind next to
in front of

3 Look and read.

You need:
a toilet roll, white paper, pink paper, glue, scissors, felt tips or coloured pencils, pipe cleaners

Cover the toilet roll with white paper.

Draw a bunny face on it.

Cut out 2 ears from the white paper and the centres from the pink paper.

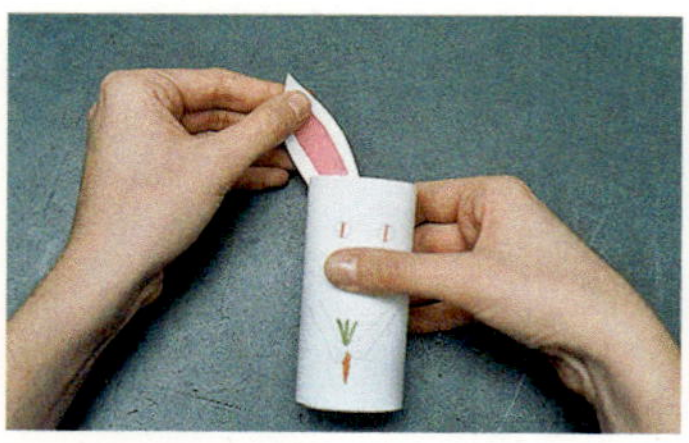

Glue on the ears.

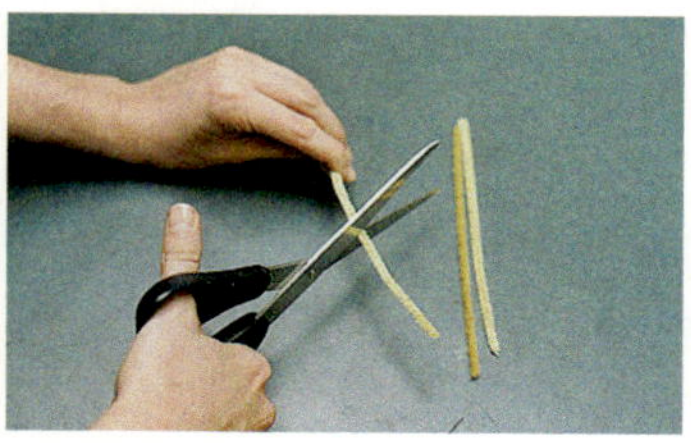

Glue on the pipe cleaners.

4 Make your own Easter egg cup.

 CD 2.36

Hello Hallo

boy Junge
girl Mädchen
children Kinder

basketball Basketball
computer game Computerspiel
inline skating Inlineskaten
picture Bild
singing Singen
skateboard Skateboard
tennis Tennis

Hello./Hi. Hallo.

Good morning. Guten Morgen.

How are you? – I'm fine, thanks.
Wie geht es dir? – Danke, gut.

What's your name? – My name is ...
Wie heißt du? – Ich heiße ...

What do you like? –
I like ... And you?
Was magst du? –
Ich mag ... Und du?

Who is it? Wer ist es?

I can see (a) ... Ich sehe (ein/e) ...

Colours and numbers
Farben und Zahlen

black schwarz
blue blau
brown braun
green grün
grey grau
orange orange
pink rosa, pink
purple lila
red rot
white weiß
yellow gelb

one eins
two zwei
three drei
four vier
five fünf
six sechs
seven sieben
eight acht
nine neun
ten zehn

What colour is it? –
It's green (blue ...).
Welche Farbe hat es? –
Es ist grün (blau ...).

What's your telephone number? –
My telephone number is ...
Wie lautet deine Telefonnummer? –
Meine Telefonnummer ist ...

At school In der Schule

(black)board Tafel
book Buch
class Klasse
classroom Klassenzimmer
computer Computer
folder Ordner
glue stick Klebestift
lollipop lady Schülerlotsin
pen Füller
pencil Bleistift
pencil case Federmäppchen
pencil sharpener Spitzer

Words

pupil Schüler
rubber Radiergummi
ruler Lineal
school Schule
schoolbag Schultasche
school things Schulsachen
school uniform Schuluniform
(a pair of) scissors eine Schere
teacher Lehrer(in)

in in
on auf
under unter

I've got a ... Ich habe ein(e, en) ...

I go to Westminster School.
Ich gehe in die Westminster-Schule.

I'm in class 3c.
Ich bin in der Klasse 3c.

My teacher is Mrs/Mr ...
Meine Lehrerin/Mein Lehrer heißt Frau/Herr ...

What about you? Und du?

Body and feelings
Körper und Gefühle

arm Arm
body Körper
ear Ohr
eye Auge
face Gesicht
finger Finger
foot – feet Fuß – Füße
hair Haar
hand Hand
head Kopf
knee Knie
leg Bein
mouth Mund
nose Nase
shoulder Schulter
toe Zeh
tooth – teeth Zahn – Zähne

angry zornig
fine gut
happy glücklich
(to) know wissen
sad traurig
scared verängstigt, erschrocken
they sie
tired müde

How do you feel? – I'm happy/sad ...
Wie fühlst du dich? – Ich bin glücklich/traurig ...

I'm okay. Mir geht's ganz gut.
I'm sorry! Es tut mir leid!

Toys Spielzeug

big groß
bike Fahrrad
car Auto
castle Burg, Schloss
children Kinder
computer game Computerspiel
doll Puppe
fish Fisch
football Fußball
guitar Gitarre
helicopter Hubschrauber
helmet Helm
horse Pferd
racing car Rennauto

small klein
spaceship Raumschiff
teddy bear Teddybär
(to) want wollen
(to) wish (for) sich wünschen

eleven elf
twelve zwölf
thirteen dreizehn
fourteen vierzehn
fifteen fünfzehn
sixteen sechzehn
seventeen siebzehn
eighteen achtzehn
nineteen neunzehn
twenty zwanzig

British britisch
euro **(€)** Euro
money Geld
penny – pence **(p)** Penny – Pence
pound **(£)** Pfund

How much is the ...? –
The ... is ... pounds.
Wie viel kostet der (die, das) ...? –
Der (die, das) ... kostet ... Pfund.

How much is it? – It's ... pounds. Wie viel kostet das? – Das macht ... Pfund.

Tim/Susan wants ...
Tim/Susan möchte ...

Clothes Kleidung

boots Stiefel
cap Kappe
coat Mantel
dress Kleid
gloves Handschuhe
jacket Jacke
(a pair of) **jeans** eine Jeans
pullover Pullover
(to) put on anziehen
scarf Schal
shirt Hemd
shoes Schuhe
(a pair of) shorts
eine kurze Hose, Shorts
skirt Rock
socks Socken
(to) take off ausziehen
(a pair of) trousers eine Hose
T-shirt T-Shirt
(to) wear tragen, anhaben
woolly hat Mütze

For my holidays, I pack ...
Für meine Ferien packe ich ... ein.

Sally puts on **her** ... / takes off **her** ...
Sally zieht ihr(e, en) ... an/aus.

Weather and days
Wetter und Tage

Monday Montag
Tuesday Dienstag
Wednesday Mittwoch
Thursday Donnerstag
Friday Freitag
Saturday Samstag
Sunday Sonntag
day Tag
week Woche

cloud/y Wolke/wolkig
cold kalt
fog/gy Nebel/neblig
hot heiß

rain/y Regen/regnerisch
snow/y Schnee/verschneit
sun/ny Sonne/sonnig
weather forecast Wettervorhersage
wind/y Wind/windig

When can we meet? – We can meet on Monday (Tuesday …). Wann können wir uns treffen? – Wir können uns am Montag (Dienstag …) treffen.

What day is it? – It's Monday. (Tuesday ...). Welchen Tag haben wir? – Es ist Montag (Dienstag ...).

What's the weather like today? – Today it's windy (sunny …).
Wie ist das Wetter heute? – Heute ist es windig (sonnig …).

On Monday, it's sunny.
Am Montag ist es sonnig.

Around the year
Rund ums Jahr

January Januar
February Februar
March März
April April
May Mai
June Juni
July Juli
August August
September September
October Oktober
November November
December Dezember
month Monat

spring Frühling
summer Sommer
autumn Herbst
winter Winter
season Jahreszeit

balloon Ballon
birthday Geburtstag
cake Torte, Kuchen
calendar Kalender
candle Kerze
card Karte
(to) come kommen
crown Krone
guest Gast
invitation Einladung
party Party, Feier
present Geschenk
weekend Wochenende
Dear … Liebe/Lieber …

When's your birthday? – My birthday is in …
Wann ist dein Geburtstag? – Mein Geburtstag ist im …

Happy birthday!
Alles Gute zum Geburtstag!

How old are you? – I'm 8 (years old).
Wie alt bist du? – Ich bin 8 (Jahre alt).

Family and friends
Familie und Freunde

aunt Tante
boy Junge
brother Bruder
family Familie

father/dad Vater/Papa
friend Freund(in)
girl Mädchen
grandfather/grandpa Großvater/Opa
grandmother/grandma Großmutter/Oma
mother/mum Mutter/Mama
sister Schwester
uncle Onkel

My best friend is ...
Mein(e) beste(r) Freund(in) ist ...

He/She is ... years old.
Er/Sie ist ... Jahre alt.

He/She has got ... Er/Sie hat ...

How many brothers/sisters have you got? – I've got .../ I haven't got ...
Wie viele Brüder/Schwestern hast du? – Ich habe ... / Ich habe keine ...

Have you got brothers or sisters?
Hast du Geschwister?

This is my family. / These are my friends.
Das ist meine Familie. / Dies sind meine Freunde.

Drinks Getränke

coffee Kaffee
coke Cola
hot chocolate Kakao
lemonade Limonade
(a glass of) milk (ein Glas) Milch
orange juice Orangensaft
(a cup of) tea (eine Tasse) Tee
water Wasser

What drinks do you like? – I like ...
Welche Getränke magst du? – Ich mag ...

I like ... best. Am liebsten mag ich ...

What drinks don't you like? – I don't like ...
Welche Getränke magst du nicht? – Ich mag kein(e, en) ...

What would you like to drink? – I'd like ..., please. Was würdest du gerne trinken? – Ich hätte gerne ..., bitte.

Breakfast Frühstück

bread Brot
breakfast Frühstück
butter Butter
cheese Käse
cornflakes Cornflakes
(to) drink trinken
(to) eat essen
egg Ei
ham Schinken
honey Honig
jam Marmelade
roll Brötchen
toast Toast

What do you have for breakfast?
Was isst/trinkst du zum Frühstück?

For breakfast, I have ...
Zum Frühstück esse/trinke ich ...

Do you like ...? – Yes, I do. / No, I don't.
Magst du ...? – Ja. / Nein.

Can I have the ..., please? – Here you are. Kann ich bitte den/die/das ... haben? – Hier, bitte.

Fruit Obst

apple Apfel
banana Banane
cherry Kirsche
fruit Frucht, Obst
lemon Zitrone
melon Melone
orange Orange, Apfelsine
pear Birne
pineapple Ananas
plum Pflaume
strawberry Erdbeere
tree Baum

(to) add hinzufügen
(to) cut schneiden
ice cream Eiskrem
ice cream stand Eisstand
jug Krug
(to) mix mischen
(to) peel schälen
(to) pour eingießen
(to) put hineingeben, legen, stellen
scoop Eiskugel
smoothie Smoothie, Fruchtshake
(to) wash waschen

What's your favourite ice cream?
Was ist dein Lieblingseis?

Can I help you?
Kann ich dir/euch/Ihnen helfen?

I'd like ... – Here you are.
Ich hätte gerne ... – Hier, bitte.

That's ... pounds, please. – Thank you.
Das macht bitte ... Pfund. – Danke.

Goodbye. Auf Wiedersehen.

Pets Haustiere

bird Vogel
budgie Wellensittich
cat Katze
dog Hund
fish Fisch(e)
guinea pig Meerschweinchen
hamster Hamster
little klein
mouse – mice Maus – Mäuse
pet Haustier
rabbit Kaninchen
tail Schwanz
tortoise Schildkröte
very sehr
wing Flügel

What's your favourite pet?
Was ist dein Lieblingshaustier?

My favourite pet is a ...
Mein Lieblingshaustier ist ein(e) ...

Its name is ... Es heißt ...

Can I help you? – I've lost my pet.
Kann ich dir/euch/Ihnen helfen? – Ich habe mein Haustier verloren.

What colour is it? – It's black (brown ...).
Welche Farbe hat es? – Es ist schwarz (braun ...).

London London

bus Bus
bus driver Busfahrer
England England
guard Wache, Wachposten
king König
(to) move bewegen, sich bewegen
palace Palast
prince Prinz
princess Prinzessin
queen Königin
Royal Family Königsfamilie
sight Sehenswürdigkeit

I want to be a … Ich will ein(e) … sein.

I want to see … Ich will … sehen.

Farm animals
Bauernhoftiere

animal Tier
barn Stall
bee Biene
clumsy ungeschickt
cow Kuh
duck Ente
farm Bauernhof
farmer Bauer
goose – geese Gans – Gänse
hen Huhn, Henne
horse Pferd
pig Schwein
sheep Schaf, Schafe

What's your favourite animal? – It's a …
Was ist dein Lieblingstier? – Es ist ein(e) …

Robin Hood Robin Hood

arrow Pfeil
bow Bogen
castle Burg, Schloss
(to) catch fangen
(to) dress up sich verkleiden
forest Wald
(to) give geben
hat Hut
(to) play a trick
einen Streich spielen
poor arm
rich reich
(to) ride (a horse)
(ein Pferd) reiten
sheriff Sheriff
(to) shoot schießen

Help! Hilfe!

Hands up! Hände hoch!

Happy Halloween
Fröhliches Halloween

bat Fledermaus
broom Besen
costume Kostüm, Verkleidung
dark dunkel
door Tür
ghost Geist, Gespenst
Halloween Halloween
hat Hut
house Haus
(to) knock klopfen
monster Ungeheuer, Monster
moon Mond
night Nacht
pumpkin Kürbis

(to) shake schütteln
skeleton Gerippe, Skelett
star Stern
sweets Süßigkeiten
witch Hexe

Happy Halloween!
Fröhliches Halloween!

It's 8 (9 …) **o'clock.**
Es ist 8 (9 …) Uhr.

Trick or treat! Süßes oder Saures!

Merry Christmas
Frohe Weihnachten

bell Glocke
carrot Karotte
chimney Schornstein
Christmas card Weihnachtskarte
Christmas Eve Heiligabend, Weihnachtsabend
Christmas tree Weihnachtsbaum
Father Christmas Weihnachtsmann
fireplace (offener) Kamin
(to) get presents Geschenke bekommen
hungry hungrig
mistletoe Mistel(zweig)
reindeer Rentier(e)
sleigh Schlitten
snowman Schneemann
stocking Strumpf

Merry Christmas! Frohe Weihnachten!

Valentine's Day
Valentinstag

Valentine's Day Valentinstag
(to) write Valentine's cards
Valentinskarten schreiben

It's Valentine's Day.
Es ist Valentinstag.

I like you. Ich mag dich.

Happy Easter Frohe Ostern

basket Korb
bush Busch
(to) colour färben, anmalen
Easter bunny Osterhase
Easter egg Osterei
Easter egg cup Ostereierbecher
fence Zaun
fun Spaß
happy glücklich
(to) hide verstecken
sad traurig
(to) share teilen

behind hinter
in in
in front of vor
next to neben
on auf
under unter

Happy Easter! Frohe Ostern!

Is the yellow (red …) egg in/on/under the ...?
Ist das gelbe (rote …) Ei in/auf/unter dem/der ...?

Der verbindliche Wortschatz ist **fett** gedruckt.